Reggie Finlayson

Lerner Publications Company
Minneapolis

This is dedicated to the lovers of freedom and justice, who endured all to achieve their aims, and to Celiwa-Zuri.

A pronunciation guide appears on page 111. The publisher wishes to thank Peter Lekgoathi for his assistance in its creation.

A&E and **BIOGRAPHY** are trademarks of the A&E Television Networks, registered in the United States and other countries.

Some of the people profiled in this series have also been featured in A&E's acclaimed BIOGRAPHY series, which is available on videocassette from A&E Home Video. Call 1-800-423-1212 to order.

Lerner Publications Company
241 First Avenue North
Minneapolis, MN 55401

Website address: www.lernerbooks.com

Library of Congress Cataloging-in-Publication Data

Finlayson, Reggie.
    Nelson Mandela / by Reggie Finlayson.
        p.   cm. — (A & E biography)
    Includes bibliographical references and index.
    Summary: Describes the childhood, political activities, imprisonment, family, and presidency of Nelson Mandela.
    ISBN 0-8225-4936-0 (alk. paper)
    1. Mandela, Nelson, 1918– —Juvenile literature. 2. Presidents—South Africa—Biography—Juvenile literature. 3. South Africa—Politics and government—1948—Juvenile literature. [1. Mandela, Nelson, 1918–2. Presidents—South Africa. 3. Civil rights workers. 4. Blacks—South Africa—Biography.]
    I. Title. II. Series.
    DT1949.M35F56   1999
    968.06'5'092
    [B]—dc21   97-50167

Manufactured in the United States of America
1 2 3 4 5 6 – JR – 04 03 02 01 00 99

CONTENTS

Nelson Mandela made history when he was sworn in as South Africa's first black president.

Chapter **ONE**

A TURNING POINT IN HISTORY

THE MORNING OF MAY 10, 1994, WAS BRIGHT and clear. Leaders from around the world had gathered in Pretoria, South Africa, for the largest international gathering ever held on the African continent. The air crackled with excitement as visitors from Europe, Asia, Africa, and America took their places. Blacks and whites sat side by side in the glistening sandstone amphitheater formed by the government buildings. Few could have imagined such a scene a decade earlier, when South Africa was locked in a titanic and violent struggle between the races. But that time was a memory that many hoped would quickly fade. The world's leaders were in Pretoria to mark the change.

The assembled leaders were indeed impressive—but

not nearly as impressive as the historic event they had come to honor. They were witnessing nothing short of the birth of a new nation.

Like a lion, Nelson Rolihlahla Mandela, newly elected president of South Africa, strode across the stage to the podium, and all eyes followed him in silence. There was a youthful spring in his step—despite his seventy-six years, despite the nearly three decades he had spent in South African prisons. He greeted the audience with open arms. It was easy to see how his name had become a rallying call, his face a symbol of survival, his spirit the very essence of freedom. As he acknowledged kings and queens, presidents and prime ministers, they leaned forward in their seats so as not to miss a word.

"Today, all of us do, by our presence here, and by our celebration in other parts of our country and the world, confer glory and hope to newborn liberty," Mandela intoned with a voice full of a strange power. It was clear, even to the most insensitive, that this was not just another inauguration speech. In his words could be heard the echo of generations of South Africans, alive and dead, who had struggled to be free. His voice seemed infused with the voices of those who had been massacred in Sharpeville and Soweto—of Steven Biko and thousands of others who had been detained, beaten, and even killed—the voices of all the restless souls who had died to change the nation.

But Mandela's words were also charged with the

compassion of a man who had known too much violence and hatred. "We have triumphed in the effort to implant hope in the breasts of the millions of our people," he said. "We enter into a covenant that we shall build the society in which all South Africans, both black and white, will be able to walk tall, without any fear in their hearts, assured of their unalienable right to human dignity—a rainbow nation at peace with itself and the world."

The audience nodded, sighed, and clapped. Mandela's own example offered hope to not only South Africans but also to the world at large. He had stood up to forces of oppression and spent more than a quarter of a century in prison for his trouble. Yet he had come out unbowed and prepared to continue the struggle. At a point in life when most men retire, Nelson Mandela took the helm of a new nation. He had traveled a long way—and crossed many famous rivers.

Rolihlahla Mandela grew up in the Transkei region of South Africa in a Xhosa village like this one.

Chapter **TWO**

BIRTH OF A LEADER

ROLIHLAHLA MANDELA WAS BORN ON JULY 18, 1918, in the small village of Mvezo in South Africa. This rural community sits in an area full of rolling hills, fertile valleys, and generous streams. It is about 800 miles east of Cape Town, 550 miles south of Johannesburg, and next to the blue waters of the Indian Ocean. This land, called the Transkei region, is the traditional homeland of the Xhosa, one of the largest ethnic groups in South Africa.

Rolihlahla was born into the Thembu clan within the Xhosa nation. From the beginning, he was steeped in the culture of this group. At birth, he was not called Nelson, the name by which he later became known. Instead, he bore the traditional Xhosa name

Rolihlahla. According to custom, Xhosa people were given names that described them in some way or suggested what they might become. Rolihlahla meant "pulling the branch of a tree." Gadla Henry Mphakanyiswa, Rolihlahla's father, gave this name to his son.

Rolihlahla was born into a royal Xhosa family. Gadla Henry Mphakanyiswa was a minor chief in the village of Mvezo. Like a mayor, he kept business moving in the village and settled disputes. When necessary, he assumed the role of judge and decided cases according to tribal law. Finally, he served as something of a prime minister, or chief adviser, to the highest tribal authority, the Thembu king.

Rolihlahla loved his father and was very proud of his experience, his wisdom, and the way people in the community looked up to him. The man provided the first lessons in leadership for his son.

"In later years, I discovered that my father was not only an adviser to kings but a king-maker," Nelson Rolihlahla Mandela later wrote in his autobiography, *Long Walk to Freedom*. He explained that in the 1920s, the Xhosa king Jongilizwe had died unexpectedly. The heir apparent had been too young to assume the throne, and a dispute had broken out over which other heir should claim the role in the interim. Rolihlahla's father took a controversial stance to support a man who was fairly low in the pecking order but who was the best educated—a man named Jongintaba.

Mphakanyiswa's opinion carried the day, and

Jongintaba was installed as acting king, or regent. The elders soon applauded the decision—and the wisdom and good fortune Jongintaba would bring to the Xhosa people. As it turned out, the choice would also make a difference for the Mandela family. But that would be years in coming.

A Legacy of Struggle

During Rolihlahla's youth, his society was changing rapidly. The old tribal ways were yielding to new ideas about religion, housing, clothing, and marriage. Many neighbors threw out the old ideas, but Rolihlahla's father held fast to the traditional way of life.

According to custom, Mphakanyiswa had four wives. Rolihlahla's mother, Nosekeni Fanny, was the third. Rolihlahla was the oldest of his mother's children but the youngest male among all his father's children. Between the four wives, Mphakanyiswa produced thirteen children: four boys and nine girls.

The entire family did not live together under one roof. Each wife had her own kraal, a rural homestead that included fields for farming, a pen for animals, and one or more thatched huts for living space. The kraals of the four wives were similar but were separated by several miles. Rolihlahla's father divided his time equally between them.

Mphakanyiswa was a proud man. He was wealthy by Xhosa standards and respected in his community. He drew pay as a local chief and enjoyed the status

A nineteenth-century Xhosa chief, Moqoma, with his four wives

that went along with it. But even a wealthy and re-spected Xhosa man did not have all that much status in South African society.

The population of South Africa was multiracial. Nearly eighty percent of the people were black and belonged to groups such as the Xhosa, Zulu, Ndebele, Sans, Venda, Swazi, and Pondo. There were also East Indians, whites, and people of mixed race. Most of the country's whites were Afrikaners, also called Boers, descendants of Dutch settlers who traced their history in South Africa back to 1652.

For centuries, the great European nations had competed for control over various parts of Africa. In

South Africa, the Dutch eventually lost out to the British. It was the British who continued to control South Africa during Rolihlahla's childhood.

The British recognized the tribal governments of the Xhosa, Zulu, and other African groups—but only in part. Local chiefs reported not only to their tribal kings but also to white magistrates appointed by the British. These magistrates had more power and status than the tribal authorities, and they had the final say in decision making.

Soon after Rolihlahla was born, his father made the mistake of acting as if he were equal in status to a white magistrate. The offended magistrate charged Mphakanyiswa with not following orders and removed him from office. There was no investigation or second chance—as there would have been for a white official. With the stroke of a pen, the magistrate stripped Rolihlahla's father of his position and livelihood.

The magistrate did not, however, take Mphakanyiswa's dignity. Nor did he strip him of pride and respect. Like all modern Xhosa, Rolihlahla's father had learned to cope with hard times. This ability came, at least in part, from a tragic event that had occurred several generations earlier. The event was called the Mfecane.

THE MFECANE

In 1857 the Xhosa were a dominant force in eastern South Africa. They had successfully fended off attacks by the British for decades. But the Mfecane, or "great

Xhosa cattle killing," would shatter the independence of the Xhosa nation.

The Mfecane began with a young woman named Nongqawuse. She was in her late teens or early twenties at the time and was training to become a shaman, or healer. As a shaman, Nongqawuse was skilled at seeing the spiritual causes of diseases and personal troubles.

One day when Nongqawuse was in the forest with her sisters, she heard a voice beckoning her. As she stepped into the bush, she saw three strange figures.

"Who are you?" Nongqawuse shouted.

"We are your ancestors," said the voice. It continued:

> Listen carefully. We have come from the land of the dead with a message. The dead ones have taken pity on the Xhosa people and, for the Xhosa people, deliverance is near. On the fourteenth day of next month great miracles shall happen in this land. On that day, the sun will rise in the east and the graves of the old chiefs will open and those chiefs will rise in the purity of youth. They shall rule the Xhosa more wisely than they did before and the ground will open like a womb and deliver thousands of cattle. There will be no more rich and poor Xhosa, for everybody will have enough. A great wind will sweep from the north and drive all the white people into the sea and the white race will plague the Xhosa race no longer.

But before this can happen, the Xhosa must purify themselves and the whole land. They must show their faith by burning the corn in the fields, killing all the cows and goats, oxen and sheep in their kraals. They must cease eating three times a day and eat only one light meal until the Day of Miracles.

Nongqawuse was speechless when her clansmen arrived just in time to see the three figures depart. One of the clansmen asked the Xhosa king to consider the message from the ancestors. Despite suspicions, the clansman persuaded the king that the instructions by the three ghosts should be followed. The slaughter of animals began almost immediately.

To say the least, there were some who resisted the slaughter, but most who did were forced to destroy their livestock and crops. There was a madness in the air as the Xhosa people killed their animals.

The real story behind the Mfecane may never be known. Some historians believe that the young woman had been tricked by white settlers or officers of the British government posing as ghosts. What is clear is that after the Mfecane, many Xhosa died of starvation and disease—but that wasn't the worst part.

In the face of the human tragedy, British governor George Grey took advantage of the situation. With the Xhosa weakened by hunger, Grey seized their land for whites and drove tens of thousands of Xhosa to work on white-owned farms. The Xhosa had always successfully resisted the British in the past. But the Mfecane broke the back of Xhosa control. The effects could still be felt during Rolihlahla Mandela's youth.

VILLAGE LIFE

Like the Xhosa as a whole, Rolihlahla's father was unable to defy British authorities. Mphakanyiswa was no longer a chief, and with the change in family income, Rolihlahla's mother opted to move her household a few miles away to a smaller village called Qunu. It was nearer to her family and gave her a greater sense of security. In the new village, occupied by just a few hundred people, Rolihlahla's mother had three huts: one for cooking, one for sleeping, and one for storage.

The huts were round structures with mud walls and angled grass roofs supported by wooden poles. The doorways were generally so low that people had to stoop to enter. The huts were set some distance from fields of corn, sorghum, beans, and pumpkins. Rolihlahla's family ate what they grew, since imported products were expensive.

Rolihlahla's family did not own their own land, however. The Native Land Act of 1913 had restricted black ownership of land in South Africa. Instead, the government owned the land on which Rolihlahla lived. In decades to come, the Native Land Act and similar codes would be used to force blacks off their own tribal lands and to strip them of even the most basic rights.

Rolihlahla's childhood, although no longer privi-
leged, was a happy one. He was a herd boy who
tended sheep and cattle. Like all Xhosa, he learned to
love cattle. He felt an almost mystical connection with
the animals that was common among his people. To
the Xhosa, cattle represented food, wealth, a source of
happiness, and a blessing from God.

Nature was Rolihlahla's main teacher, and he ab-
sorbed its many lessons. He learned to gather wild
honey, to identify edible wild plants, to catch fish with
twine and a piece of wire, and to hunt birds with a
slingshot. In a time-honored fashion, older herd boys
taught Rolihlahla the Xhosa version of a martial art—
stick fighting.

Like these young men, Rolihlahla became skilled at stick fighting.

Rural life did much to strengthen Rolihlahla's body and sharpen his senses. But it was the traditional Thembu and other Xhosa tales that sparked his imagination and showed him the difference between right and wrong. Rolihlahla listened as the older herd boys told fantastic myths and sat in awe when professional storytellers weaved tales of heroism, sacrifice, and passion. Rolihlahla's favorite stories chronicled the ancient times of the first people in the land.

Qunu was a tightly knit community where people related to one another more as family than as neighbors. Though whites seldom entered this world, the local government representative was white and so was the owner of the nearest store. Occasionally, white travelers and white policemen passed through the small village, but they were rare visitors.

LEARNING NEW LESSONS

Most of the villagers in Qunu were Xhosa, but there were also some Mfengu, an ethnic group that had migrated into Xhosa territory in the early nineteenth century. Nearly a hundred years later, the Mfengu still lived as a people apart in the land of the Xhosa. Their hosts often looked down on them. Without their own tribal lands, they were at first forced to do the jobs no others would.

Gradually, however, the Mfengu began to pursue European-style education, to master English, and to adopt a western style of dress and housing. They eventually became clergymen, policemen, teachers, and clerks—all relatively well-paid positions. Their success did not make the Mfengu any more popular with the Xhosa. There was some hostility, resentment, and prejudice between the two groups.

Rolihlahla's father had a different attitude from most of the Xhosa, however. He judged people on their actions rather than on their ethnic origins. He urged his son to do the same, but not just in words. Rolihlahla watched his father form bonds of friendship across ethnic and religious divides. One such friendship, formed with a Mfengu man, would have a profound effect on Rolihlahla's early life.

Ben Mbekela, a retired Mfengu teacher, noticed Rolihlahla's curiosity and intelligence. He told Rolihlahla's parents that their son might have a bright future if he were educated in one of the newly established Methodist schools near the village. Though no one in the family had ever attended school, Rolihlahla's father took to the idea immediately. At age seven, Rolihlahla enrolled in the local Methodist school.

Attending school was quite an adjustment. Rolihlahla stepped into a strange new world that forced him to change the language he spoke and the clothes he wore. Gone was his traditional dress—a piece of cloth wrapped around his body. In its place, Rolihlahla wore a pair of his father's cutoff pants, a piece of string as a belt, and a western-style shirt. The other students, who came from wealthier families, poked fun at the new student. But Rolihlahla felt no shame. He was proud to wear his father's oversized pants.

Rolihlahla even received a new name. His teacher, Miss Mdingane, politely told him that his new name was Nelson and that this was the name he would answer to in school. Nobody knows why the teacher chose Nelson. Maybe she was thinking of the British naval captain, Lord Horatio Nelson. There was no way to know for sure. Unlike African names, English names did not come with meanings and tales.

Nelson first assumed he was renamed because Europeans had trouble pronouncing African names. But later he wondered if there had been some other reason. He noticed that African history was absent from his studies and that students were encouraged to think of African ways as backward. He wondered if there was a connection between these ideas and his new English name.

This was a time of wondering and difficult lessons. When Nelson was nine, his father arrived unexpectedly at his mother's home. Mphakanyiswa usually divided his time evenly between the households of his four wives. The schedule was fairly routine. So Nelson and his mother were surprised when Mphakanyiswa showed up several days early. They were also surprised by how sick Mphakanyiswa looked. He had lost weight and coughed violently, almost without stopping. He complained about his lungs. Like many Xhosa people, Mphakanyiswa had a great passion for smoking, and his health problems were likely a result of this habit.

Nelson's mother, with the help of the youngest co-wife, did what she could to care for Mphakanyiswa. Nothing could relieve the hacking cough, however—until Mphakanyiswa called for his wife to fetch his tobacco and pipe. The two wives hesitated out of fear that smoking would only make the man's condition worse. Still, Rolihlahla's father insisted, and the wives finally gave in. Mphakanyiswa took a deep draw on the pipe, stopped coughing, and was suddenly calm. For another hour or so, he continued to smoke. Then, with the pipe still lit, he quietly died.

The elders claimed it was a blessing for a man to die so peacefully. But at age nine, Nelson could only grieve the loss of his father. It was his father who had provided him with his sense of identity. His father had defined him. With his father gone, Nelson's life changed drastically.

Chief Jongintaba, above, *became Nelson's guardian after Mphakanyiswa's death.*

Chapter **THREE**

IN THE ROYAL KRAAL

SHORTLY AFTER MPHAKANYISWA'S FUNERAL, Nelson's mother told him that he was to leave Qunu. The news was something of a shock, but Nelson didn't question her about where he was going or why. African children did not question their elders. Nelson simply packed a few items and prepared to go.

He and his mother started out early in the day. The morning sun gave the village a warm glow. As they climbed a hill overlooking Qunu, Nelson studied the houses, fields, and surrounding forest. He wondered if he would ever see his home again, and he tried hard to burn the scene into his memory. He thought about his friends herding cattle, stick fighting, and playing in the forest. He already missed them.

Nelson and his mother walked all day, mostly in silence. Then, late in the afternoon, they entered a valley that contained a village. In the center was a compound more impressive than anything he'd ever seen. In structure, the buildings reminded Nelson of the huts in his mother's village. But the fine thatched roofs seemed incredibly high. The walls were whitewashed and gleamed in the sun. The buildings had a look of elegance that was unfamiliar to Nelson. Nearby, there were neatly tended gardens, fertile fields, fruit trees, and herds of cattle and sheep.

Nelson's eyes grew wide with wonder as he watched several men step from fine luxury cars that had pulled into the village. Among the group was a stocky, dark-skinned man who came toward the two travelers with his hand extended. He was Jongintaba—regent of the Thembu tribe of the Xhosa nation.

Jongintaba! His name meant "one who looks at the mountain." This was the man Nelson's father had supported so many years before—a man who would repay that act with countless acts of kindness. Mother and son were warmly received and together enjoyed the hospitality of the village for a few days—long enough for Nelson to settle in. This was to be his new home.

Nelson missed his mother when she left but quickly adjusted to his new surroundings. Jongintaba and his wife treated Nelson like their own son. He was like a brother to the regent's two children, especially to the

Nelson lived in this hut under Jongintaba's care.

regent's son, Justice. He ate with the family, slept in their house, and was respected by visitors.

Nelson's new home was the center of tribal government for the Thembu. The regent called meetings as needed, and discussions focused on issues like drought, caring for cattle, and new laws or policies. All tribal members were welcome, and every man was given the chance to speak, regardless of his station in life. The men talked and argued until everyone agreed.

Nelson attended the meetings and listened carefully. He particularly enjoyed the heated discussions that preceded any decision or action. This was African democracy at work. "Democracy meant all men were to be heard, and a decision was taken together as a people," Nelson would later write in his autobiography. "Majority rule was a foreign notion. A minority was not to be crushed by a majority."

In later years, Nelson would remember what took place in the royal kraal and it would affect his own

Nelson loved hearing stories about his ancestors' battles. In the nineteenth century, Xhosa ambushed British soldiers, above.

leadership style. The system had flaws, but there was something of value there as well. Watching the process at work sharpened Nelson's interest in history and the ways in which people might work together.

Visiting chiefs fascinated Nelson. Many were wise and well spoken. Nelson was particularly impressed by an elderly man named Chief Zwelibhangile Joyi. The chief loved to tell stories about the heroes of the past. Although old and quite wrinkled, he seemed to swell with youthful power when he recalled the courage of the Xhosa warriors who stood against the powerful nineteenth-century British army. The chief also talked about the ancient ancestors of the Xhosa who had lived in the great lakes region of east-central Africa. Nelson loved to sit and listen to these tales.

STEPPING STONES TO MANHOOD

Without Nelson realizing it, he was being groomed to fill a role his father had held before him—adviser to the king. By the time he was sixteen, Nelson had become an impressive young man. But he was not yet an adult in the traditional or tribal sense. The rite of circumcision would make him an adult in the eyes of the community.

Circumcision, the cutting of a young man's foreskin, is a minor operation. But more important than the actual procedure was the transmission of Xhosa values and the sense of group unity. Leading up to the operation and during the period of recovery, boys received instruction on what it meant to be an adult in Xhosa society. A similar ceremony took place for girls, but without any physical operation.

Following the circumcision, Nelson and other young men his age rested in secluded huts until their wounds properly healed. Afterward, the huts were burned to the ground with all the contents inside. The boys' last links to childhood were destroyed, and they were considered men. According to tradition, Nelson also received a circumcision name. It was Dalibunga, which roughly translated means "the founder of the rulers of the Transkei."

Finally, with great fanfare, Nelson and the other young men were presented to the tribe as full-fledged members. The ceremony was like a high school graduation, a cotillion, and a birthday party all rolled into

one. Villagers watched as the young men were presented to society. Proud parents showered their children with gifts, and Nelson was as proud as anyone
to take his place in the adult world of his people.

Among the many people who spoke that day was a
man named Chief Meligqili. He stood and surveyed
the throng that had gathered. Then he looked at the
young men and started to speak:

> There sit our sons; young, healthy, and hand-
> some, the flower of the Xhosa tribe, the pride of
> our nation. We have just circumcised them in a
> ritual that promises them manhood, but I am
> here to tell you that it is an empty, illusory
> promise, a promise that can never be fulfilled.
> For we Xhosas, and all black South Africans are
> a conquered people.

Suddenly, the mood shifted. What had started as a
purely joyous occasion turned somber. Smiles fell
away from the faces of parents and children alike.
They clearly did not want to hear this kind of talk,
but the old man pressed on:

> We are slaves in our own country. We are tenants
> on our own soil. We have no strength, no power,
> no control over our own destiny in the land of
> our birth. [The young men] will go to cities
> where they will live in shacks and drink cheap

alcohol all because we have no land to give them where they could prosper and multiply. They will cough their lungs out deep in the bowels of the white man's mines, destroying their health, never seeing the sun, so that the white man can live a life of unequaled prosperity. Among these young men are chiefs who will never rule because we have no power to govern ourselves; soldiers who will never fight for we have no weapons to fight with; scholars who will never teach because we have no place for them to study. The abilities, intelligence, the promise of these young men will be squandered in their attempt to eke out a living doing the simplest, most mindless chores for the white man. The gifts today are for naught, for we cannot give them the greatest gift of all, which is freedom and independence.

As the words washed over Nelson, he felt an intense anger toward the speaker. This was to have been one of the happiest days of his life, and this man had ruined it with his ranting. Nelson wished those foul words had never been spoken, and tried to flush them from his mind. But the words had seeped into his soul, where they began to work on him.

Nelson would later look back on that ceremony and realize that his childhood had ended then not only in a physical and social fashion. His childish notions about the political world were also beginning to fall away.

At nineteen, Nelson already showed signs of leadership.

Chapter **FOUR**

GOING TO
SCHOOL

AT AGE SIXTEEN, **N**ELSON CONTINUED HIS FORMAL
education. That was something of a luxury for African
children, who often received only a few years of
schooling before taking menial jobs. But Mandela was
not destined for working in the mines or a white
farmer's field. He was to be the advisor to kings.

He enrolled in Clarkebury Boarding Institute, one of
the best schools for black youths in southern Africa.
Children from many of the region's prominent families attended. They were often well educated and so-
phisticated. As the regent's ward, Nelson was used to
getting respect. He quickly discovered that he no
longer stood out, however. Nearly everyone in his
school had prestige in their home villages.

Although he thought of himself as nearly grown when he left home, Nelson realized that he was something of a yokel. He lost confidence in himself and tried to fit in with the more refined students. In the end, however, he learned it was best to be himself. Ability in his schoolwork was ultimately what mattered most.

All and all, his time at the school was a good experience that laid a firm foundation for future studies. More than anything, he learned that the world was a much bigger place than he had imagined. He carried that feeling with him when he graduated from Clarkebury and went on to a school named Healdtown, located in Fort Beaufort.

The school was built on the site of a nineteenth-century British fort that had served as an important outpost during the war against the Xhosa. But by the time Nelson arrived there in 1937, there were no open signs of war. The cluster of structures that formed the campus overlooked a beautiful valley. The buildings were covered with ivy, and tree-lined paths crisscrossed between them. Healdtown was a coed institution with more than a thousand black students.

Healdtown's principal, Dr. Arthur Wellington, was a proud descendant of the Duke of Wellington, a famous English general. Dr. Wellington was very British and thought that the world needed more Englishmen. He set about producing black Englishmen at the school. "We were taught—and believed—that the best ideas were English ideas, the best government was English government, and the best men were English-men," Nelson later said.

Though the school was more tolerant than some other European institutions, the instructors still made the same assumption—that Africans were backward. This attitude helped to create a sense of inferiority on the part of the students.

Even with its flaws, Healdtown did produce disciplined scholars. Students were up at 6:00 A.M. and continued their academic day until 5:00 P.M. They were expected to be in their rooms by 9:30 P.M., and their weekday evenings consisted of dinner, an hour break, and two hours of study hall. This was a rigorous schedule, but it did a lot to develop the mental muscles of the students.

The college, which was comparable to a high school in the American system, attracted students from many different parts of South Africa. Nelson met people from Basutoland, Swaziland, and Bechuanaland. There was friction between the Xhosa and other tribes. Even with his father's example, Mandela still carried some negative feelings about other ethnic groups.

Nelson did well in school. He also participated in athletics and became a good long-distance runner on the track team. In his second year, Mandela took up boxing. It was the start of a lifelong passion.

In his final year, Nelson became a prefect, an honor bestowed on students who excelled in academics or showed leadership abilities. He was proud of this accomplishment. Still, the high point of the year came later, toward the end of the term, when the school was visited by Samuel Krune Mqhayi. Mqhayi was a poet who had written part of the South African national anthem, *Nkosi Sikelel' iAfrika*. The first verse and chorus of the song had been written in 1897 by Enoch Sontonga, a Xhosa teacher. In 1927, Mqhayi added seven more verses.

When Mqhayi spoke at Nelson's school, his words shocked the students. "We cannot allow these foreigners who do not care for our culture to take over our nation," Mqhayi warned. "I predict that one day, the forces of African society will achieve a momentous victory."

The words awakened something in Nelson. They made him think of the regent's royal kraal, the heroes brought to life by Chief Joyi's tales, even the disturbing words spoken at the circumcision rites. The words were magical. When the poet moved, all eyes followed. The students' spirits rose and fell to the sound Mqhayi's voice.

When the poet finished speaking, the students stood with thunderous applause. Nelson felt himself touched in a deep way. Like many students, he had come to doubt the ability of Africans to compete with Europeans. But Mqhayi made Nelson remember the great power of his own roots. He had never felt any prouder to be Xhosa than at that moment. It was his first step toward becoming a freedom fighter.

At University College of Fort Hare in the early 1940s, Nelson Mandela was among South Africa's most promising young minds.

HIGHER LEARNING

In 1940, as World War II raged in Europe, twenty-one-year-old Nelson Mandela began his first year at the all-black University College of Fort Hare. He arrived in a sleek, double-breasted gray suit, a gift from Jongintaba. The school was a small, highly regarded college patterned after Oxford in England. There were only 150 students, and they were among the brightest in southern Africa.

Nelson had long dreamed of this day. He believed education was the key to success in the modern world, and Fort Hare was the finest institution available to a Xhosa man of his era. Since a number of other students had been his schoolmates before, he felt at home there. Many students were new to him, but they seemed to be kindred spirits. Among them was Oliver Tambo, who was destined to become a lifelong friend and partner of Nelson's. He also met some of the greatest minds on the African continent at that time. He studied with such outstanding African professors as Z. K. Matthews and D. D. T. Jabavu.

From the start, Nelson planned to study law, in preparation for his role as tribal advisor. In his first year, his studies included Roman Dutch law and Native Administration—a class that focused on laws affecting Africans. Many of these laws were intended to keep blacks and whites apart.

At the time, Nelson believed race relations were getting better in his country. World War II had something to do with his sentiment. During the war, South Africa fought against the racism of Nazi Germany. Nelson and other black thinkers assumed it was just a matter of time before South Africans would fight against racism at home, too.

But when Nelson met fellow students Nyathi Khongisa and Paul Mahabane, he began to change his mind. Khongisa and Mahabane had reputations as rebels, and they introduced Nelson to the African National Congress (ANC). Nelson had heard of the organization but knew little about it.

He learned that the ANC had been established in 1912

to work for racial equality in South Africa. Its members were mostly middle-class urban blacks and royal members of tribal society. The group had a lot in common with the National Association for the Advancement of Colored People (NAACP), established around the same time in the United States. It stressed peaceful protest, dialogue between whites and blacks, and education about the plight of black South Africans.

In 1914, two years after the African National Congress was formed, several ANC leaders visited Britain to put their concerns before the British government and public.

Exposure to the ANC changed the way Nelson thought about himself. He stopped looking at himself as simply a Xhosa man and began to see himself as an African. The ANC helped turn him into an activist who was ready to do battle against injustice where and when he saw it.

His new attitude eventually brought him into conflict with the school administration. Fort Hare students wanted a stronger voice in the running of their school, and to protest, Nelson and several others launched a boycott of student government elections. That boycott resulted in the students' expulsion from school.

Country Boy, City Man

The ride back to the royal kraal was a troubling one. Nelson knew that Jongintaba would be displeased with his expulsion. Jongintaba expected Nelson to complete his degree and become an advisor to the tribal king. Nelson did not look forward to explaining his expulsion to the older man. He approached his home like a condemned man, torn between the desire to stall and the desire to be done with the confrontation as quickly as possible.

During the initial meeting, Jongintaba did not shout. He didn't have to. With a tone of authority Nelson found difficult to resist, Jongintaba simply ordered him to do what was necessary to resume his education. There was no sense in arguing, so Nelson simply agreed and left the matter alone for the time being.

Despite the early unpleasantness, things returned to normal for Nelson at the royal kraal. He ran errands for Jongintaba and looked after some of his affairs. It was life as he had known it since he left his mother's home at age nine. The dress, conversations, and schedules were the same. Yet, Nelson saw life much differently. He realized that he had changed. He was no longer the country boy who had left for school years before.

Shortly after Nelson's return, Jongintaba announced that he was getting old and needed to put his affairs in order. At the top of his list was the well-being of his son, Justice, and his ward, Nelson. As part of his plan, Jongintaba had even chosen a wife for Nelson and had already made arrangements for the wedding.

Nelson was horrified. He knew the young woman who had been chosen. She was pleasant enough, but Nelson did not love her. More to the point, he was not ready to settle down. There was too much of the world left to explore. Nelson had been raised to respect his elders, but he was not willing to accept an arranged marriage. He considered himself a modern African man and an arranged marriage was not a modern idea. He took the only other path available to him—or so it seemed at the time—and that was to run.

Nelson did not only run away from something he disliked. He also ran toward his destiny—to a place called Johannesburg.

Johannesburg in 1946 was a large, industrialized city.

Chapter **FIVE**

JOHANNESBURG

A **WAVE OF PEOPLE MOVED INTO JOHANNESBURG** and other South African cities in the early 1940s. There were few jobs in the black villages, so young blacks, especially men, headed to the cities and surrounding mines. Nelson Mandela was one of them.

Johannesburg was big and crowded, and Nelson's head craned this way and that to take in all the tall buildings. He dodged traffic and navigated the dangers of big city nights. Many things shocked him, but none more than the great difference between the lives of whites and blacks.

Rich white suburbs, scattered throughout the city, were a world apart from the shantytowns, or townships, to which black people were restricted. The shantytowns were overcrowded, unsanitary, and lacking electricity, tarred roads, or telephones. Violence and family breakdowns were common, but no more common than police raids. Seeing these towns gave Mandela a sort of education he had not found at the schools of his youth.

Mandela needed work, and his best bet seemed to be in the mines. South Africa had huge deposits of coal, gold, and diamonds, and the mines employed many blacks. Mandela took a job as a security guard at a large gold mine. It was a good job compared with working a mile underground, where cave-ins were a constant threat and miners faced health risks from breathing dust from the digging operations.

He moved into the sprawling black shantytown of Alexandria. Though the shantytown was poor, the energy of the place was something Mandela would remember fondly for decades. He was amazed by his people's ability to find happiness and dignity in the midst of poverty and squalor.

NEW TEACHERS

Alexandria was a magnet that attracted all sorts of black people. Some were criminals. Most were poor people just trying to survive. A few were caring leaders who had the welfare of their people at heart. Among this last group was a man who would have a powerful influence on Mandela. That man was Walter Sisulu.

Mandela lived in a Johannesburg shantytown like this one.

Like Mandela, Sisulu came from the Transkei region. He was several years older than Mandela and had also worked in the mines. He was one of the lucky few who had moved on to a better job. He had become a real estate agent who handled the few parcels of land still available to blacks in Johannesburg.

Mandela impressed Sisulu from the start. The older man offered Mandela a job with a modest salary and commission. In taking the job, Mandela also shared his plans—to complete his bachelor's degree and to become a lawyer.

South Africa was a hard place for blacks to live and an even harder place for blacks to develop professional skills. Sisulu knew how valuable an education would be to Mandela. He was like a father to the younger man and supported his efforts to finish his degree through correspondence courses.

Sisulu also introduced Mandela to the law firm of Witkin, Sidelsky and Eidelman. It was one of the largest firms in Johannesburg and handled many real estate deals involving blacks. The firm was considered liberal, although that did not stop it from charging much higher rates to black clients than to white ones. Still, the firm was willing to hire a black clerk who was working on his degree. Many other firms would not hire a black under any circumstances.

For good reason, Mandela was very excited. On his first day at work, he met most of the staff. They welcomed him and treated him with more respect than whites usually gave blacks. Mandela was particularly impressed with Lazar Sidelsky, a partner in the firm. He seemed genuinely concerned with the plight of black Africans.

Sidelsky thought education was the key to black progress in South Africa. He felt that an educated man like Mandela could do much to uplift the whole race. At the very least, successful black people would provide role models for others, Sidelsky thought. He was quick to point out that Mandela had the potential to be such a role model.

At first Mandela agreed with that point of view, but he later changed his mind. When he got to know another staff member some days later, he realized that a few successful black professionals would not make much difference in the big picture of racial injustice.

Gaur Radebe, the other black clerk in the firm, had been away on business during Mandela's first day. He did, however, seek out the new man upon his return. Radebe was a stocky Zulu man, about ten years older than Mandela. He knew three languages, English, Sotho, and his native Zulu, and he expressed himself well in all of them.

Radebe was also a proud, capable man who spoke his mind freely. He believed he was equal to any man and encouraged Mandela to think the same. While Sidelsky and the other partners taught Mandela the fine points of the law, it was Radebe who taught him the facts of life. "You people stole our land from us and enslaved us," Radebe once said to some white staff members gathered informally. "Now you make us pay through the nose to get the worst pieces of it back."

Mandela discovered just how true those words were. Despite little actual work on the real estate sales, law firms routinely got most of the profits while the black agents received mere crumbs. His own firm, in working with Sisulu's real estate company, always took the lion's share of commissions made on the properties.

On one occasion, Mandela returned to Sidelsky's office after running some errands. Radebe was there. He looked at the younger clerk thoughtfully then turned to Sidelsky, who was seated behind the desk. "Look, you sit there like a lord whilst my chief [Mandela] runs around doing errands for you," he said. "The situation should be reversed, and one day it will, and we will dump all of you into the sea."

Mandela was shocked by the boldness of the statement, but Sidelsky simply shook his head and did not respond. Later he told Mandela that law and politics did not mix and warned him to stay away from "troublemakers" such as Gaur Radebe and Walter Sisulu.

After taking correspondence courses at the University of South Africa, Mandela received his bachelor's degree in 1942. Soon after, he enrolled in law school at the University of Witwatersrand. He continued to work for the law firm as a clerk. Meanwhile, Gaur Radebe and Walter Sisulu continued to educate him with their thoughts on racial equality.

Mandela flirted briefly with the Communist Party, a group that believed that all factories, land, and property should be owned in common by everyone in a nation. But Mandela never became a member of the party. He worried that a political organization dominated by whites would not be sensitive to the concerns of black people. Still, he was interested in finding a way to express his feelings about the political injustices in South Africa.

INTO THE ANC

It was through his friendship with Walter Sisulu that Mandela finally joined the African National Congress. But Mandela did not simply become a member. He became a force within the thirty-year-old organization.

At the time, there was an international groundswell to throw off the yoke of colonialism—the ruling of one nation by another, far-off nation. India was in a state of turmoil as its people pushed for the end of British rule. Similar sparks were flying in the French colonies of Southeast Asia. Africans were starting to demand and win their freedom from European powers, too.

Anton Lembede, one of Africa's leading scholars, wrote about self-rule in an African newspaper. He explained how powerful nations spent huge sums of money to keep their colonies from breaking free. He also explained how some native people were used as pawns by the ruling class. Native people who became educated professionals, Lembede said, often accepted and supported the laws of foreign rulers, instead of fighting against them.

This article caused Mandela to rethink his education and his place in the struggle for freedom. He resolved not to be used as a pawn by white authorities. Instead, he and others began to commit themselves to the ANC. In 1944, Mandela, Anton Lembede, Walter Sisulu, Oliver Tambo, and others formed the Youth League of the ANC. Their goal was the establishment of real democracy in South Africa. They would work

Mandela, right, and Walter Sisulu address an ANC Youth League meeting.

for political representation for South Africans of all races, the fair distribution of land, good education for all, the removal of restrictions on black trade unions, and the end of discriminatory laws.

Lembede was elected president of the Youth League, while Tambo became secretary and Sisulu treasurer. Mandela served on the Executive Committee. The ANC had always tried to work with the white authorities, but the Youth League pushed instead for black independence and self-rule. The league discouraged white participation, arguing that white members would undermine African self-reliance.

During the league's formative stages, members spent a lot of time planning and working out the details of their organization. Meetings took place in the home of Walter Sisulu. He and his wife, Albertina, were like the parents many of the young men had left behind. There was plenty of food at the house and always a bed for those in need.

Mandela spent a lot of time at the Sisulu home, engaging in discussions or just enjoying the company. But politics wasn't the only pastime at the house. For Mandela, love blossomed there, too. In 1944, he met a girl from rural Transkei. Evelyn Mase was a shy, pretty girl who seemed a bit overwhelmed by the fast pace of the Sisulu household. She was training to be a nurse and lived in nearby Orlando with her brother.

Nelson was touched by Evelyn's quiet beauty, and he began dating her. Their romance progressed quickly.

Nelson and Evelyn married in 1944.

Within a year, they were married in a civil ceremony. It was a far different ceremony than Nelson would have had in the royal kraal. The pomp and prestige of his early life were little more than memories now, but he did not regret the choices he had made. He was happy with his life despite the hardships.

As a black couple, Nelson and Evelyn faced the challenge of finding a decent house in Johannesburg. That was not easy. Blacks were restricted to certain areas of the city. Eventually, the couple found a small home in West Orlando, part of the township of Soweto. There they started a family. Their first child, born in 1946, was a boy named Madiba Thembelike Mandela. Within a decade, the couple would have two more children: a son named Makgatho and a daughter, Mkakaziwe, who died when she was just nine months old. All the while, Mandela not only continued his work with the ANC, he intensified it.

The South African government used passbooks to regulate the movement of blacks within the country.

Chapter **SIX**

A
REVOLUTIONARY
SPIRIT

WORLD WAR II IN EUROPE ENDED IN 1945
with the destruction of Hitler's Nazi army. Black
South Africans had participated in the war effort.
They were proud to help bring an end to the racism
of the Nazi regime. Next they wanted to see racism
stamped out in their own country. ANC leaders, particularly in the Youth League, were optimistic. Now
they could achieve their own goals, or so they
thought. As it turned out, they were wrong. Two
events taught them something they would not forget.

By this time South Africa was an independent nation
enjoying a peaceful relationship with England. Yet
whites still governed South Africa and imposed oppressive policies on others. In 1946, Prime Minister

Jan Smut passed the Asiatic Land Tenure Act. It was nicknamed "the Ghetto Act" because it restricted the movement of East Indian people in South Africa and limited them to certain ghettos, or neighborhoods. The action was a sharp reminder that discrimination was still alive and was not restricted to the blacks of the country.

The Indian community responded with a wave of protests. They continued their campaign for two years, and many of the movement's leaders landed in jail. The ANC leadership was greatly impressed by this effort. Inspired by the Indian leaders, the ANC heads no longer feared going to prison in the struggle for black civil rights.

Another event that year—a mine workers strike—added to their sense of resolve. Mining was one of South Africa's largest industries and was responsible for much of the nation's wealth. But mining also exploited the Africans who worked in the mines. Mining was dangerous, health-threatening work, for which blacks were paid a fraction of the wages of their white counterparts. Discontentment among the workers had been brewing for years, but in 1946 it came to a head.

Calling for a wage of ten shillings a day, a two-week paid vacation a year, and decent housing for workers and their families, 70,000 miners went on strike. The strike was led by J. B. Marks, president of the mine workers union; Gaur Radebe; and Moses Kotane. All were members of the ANC and the Communist Party.

Prime Minister Daniel Malan of the Nationalist party took racism and oppression to new heights.

Though the strike was nonviolent, it was illegal, and the government sent a small army of police with rifles, bayonets, and batons against the strikers. Within a week, at least nine miners had been killed and 1,248 others had been injured. The strike was brutally crushed, and Marks, Kotane, and fifty-two others were jailed. It was a sign of things to come.

THE NATIONALISTS

Soon things went from bad to worse for black South Africans. By law, non-whites—eighty percent of the country's population—were barred from voting in elections. In 1948, the country's white voters put the Nationalist Party into office. It took up the reigns of power under the leadership of Prime Minister Daniel Malan.

Malan and many other Nationalists were Afrikaners who were hostile to the English. Some Nationalists had even supported Germany during World War II. The Nationalists were particularly hateful toward blacks. They warned about what they called the *swart gevaar,* or "black threat." During the campaign, the

Nationalists had repeatedly shouted, *"Die kaffer op sy plek"* (the nigger in his place) and *"Die koelies uit die land"* (the coolies out of the country). The word coolie was an insulting term for anyone from Asia, including those from India.

Nationalist Party ideas could be grouped under one word, *apartheid*. It was a word few in the outside world had heard before. Apartheid means "apartness"—separation of the races. Some people claimed apartheid would help preserve the many cultures in South Africa, including the small tribal groups. Few took that explanation seriously, however. Most observers saw apartheid for what it was: a new word for the old idea of white supremacy.

Malan wasted no time in implementing the system of racial discrimination he championed. In 1950, his government passed two laws that stood at the very heart of apartheid. The first was the Population Registration Act, which labeled everyone in South Africa according to race. The second was the Group Areas Act, which forced different racial groups to live in different places.

In 1951, the government passed two more infamous laws. The Separate Representation of Voters Act transferred mixed-race, or "colored" South Africans to separate voting rolls. Under this system, colored South Africans could vote. But their votes did not carry much weight. Representatives they elected had no direct voice in government. That same year, the government abolished the Native Representation Council, a government advisory panel made up of black representatives.

Attitudes toward blacks, coloreds, and Indians hardened significantly during this period. Apartheid brought restriction in every area of work, schooling, housing, and family life. Nelson Mandela would later describe the system:

> An African child is born in an Africans Only hospital, taken home in an Africans Only bus, lives in an Africans Only area, and attends Africans Only schools, if he attends school at all.
>
> When he grows up, he can hold Africans Only jobs, rent a house in Africans Only townships, ride Africans Only trains and be stopped any time of the day or night and be ordered to produce a pass, failing which he will be arrested and thrown in jail. His life is circumscribed by racist laws and regulations that cripple his growth, dim his potential, and stunt his life.

By 1952, the Nationalist government was well on its way to cementing its dream of a segregated society in which Afrikaners dominated all other ethnic groups. Party members were filled with near-religious fervor. It had been 300 years since the Boer founding father, Jan van Riebeeck, had established a colony in the region. The Afrikaners took their ability to survive for three centuries as a sign that they were God's chosen people. They set about securing their victory by out-lawing nearly every legal form of protest.

Mayibuye Afrika: Let Africa Return

By 1952 Nelson Mandela was president of the ANC Youth League, and he wanted a change in tactics. As Afrikaners celebrated their tricentennial, the ANC drafted a letter to Prime Minister Malan. In it, they explained that they had exhausted all constitutional means of achieving rights for the black population. They demanded a repeal of the unjust laws that formed the basis of apartheid. If no action was taken, the organization would have to resort to extra-constitutional measures.

Malan's reply made it clear that his government had no intention of meeting the ANC's demands. The prime minister stressed his desire to preserve white rule in South Africa and promised to use force if necessary to quell any black unrest. "We regarded Malan's curt dismissal of our demands as a declaration of war," Mandela wrote in his autobiography. "We had no alternative but to resort to civil disobedience, and we embarked on preparations for mass action in earnest." That was the start of the Defiance Campaign.

On June 26, 1952, ANC leadership called for a national strike. Blacks, Indians, and coloreds marched through areas marked "Whites Only" and refused to carry passbooks that designated their racial status. Malan was as good as his word and met the strikers with mass arrests and police brutality. Mandela, Sisulu, and others were arrested.

But the strikers continued their efforts throughout the remainder of the year. The oppressed people of the country had awakened and did not plan another slumber. Walter Sisulu seemed to speak for many involved in the campaign when he made a statement upon his arrest.

"As long as I enjoy the confidence of my people, and as long as there is a spark of life and energy in me, I shall fight with courage and determination for the abolition of discriminatory laws and for the freedom of all South Africans," he said. He spent a week in jail rather than pay the fines that would have gotten him out immediately.

The Defiance Campaign was largely nonviolent. In fact, international observers commented repeatedly on the peaceful nature of the protests. Yet confrontations sometimes did turn violent, often in response to police brutality. In New Brighton in October 1952, for instance, a white policeman shot two blacks who were suspected of theft. A crowd reacted angrily, and the policeman pumped more than twenty bullets into the charging mass before escaping. People continued their rampage, and before peace returned, seven blacks and four whites were dead. Another twenty-seven people were injured. The government used this example of unrest as an excuse to clamp down even harder on the Defiance Campaign.

In addition to arresting thousands of protesters, the government "banned" more than fifty strike leaders. Under South African law, a banned person was restricted from traveling, making public appearances, speaking with other banned individuals, and participating in many other activities. By December 1952, arrests, bannings, and other government actions had halted the Defiance Campaign.

Mandela, Sisulu, and others were placed on trial as

Crowds gathered in the streets to launch the Defiance Campaign of 1952.

These protesters took over a train compartment designated for whites, and they rode into Cape Town. They were arrested upon arrival.

Communists. However, the courts refused to convict the men on the most serious charges of antigovernment activity. They were given nine-month suspended sentences, which amounted to little more than slaps on the wrist.

The movement had gained ground. The ANC had succeeded in creating a united front against apartheid. It had focused world attention on the injustices in

South Africa and had sprung into prominence. Membership increased greatly.

Yet, while Mandela and the other leaders celebrated these successes, the government in the capital city of Pretoria launched a defiance campaign of its own. Without a trial or formal charges, the government issued expanded banning orders against the bulk of the ANC leadership. It also declared that protesters could be whipped, jailed for up to three years, fined the equivalent of nearly $1,000, or be given any two of these penalties combined. Encouraging protest was punishable by an additional two years in prison or the equivalent of $500 in fines. These rulings forced the ANC to reconsider its strategy.

Practicing Law

Mandela managed to complete his law degree, despite the Defiance Campaign and his other work with the ANC. He had quit his job at Witkin, Sidelsky and Gidelman and had gained experience working for several other white law firms. He was shocked by the fact that even the most reputable firms charged black clients far more than whites. There were no black law firms in the area, so Mandela decided to start one.

In August 1952, he went out on his own. Within a short time, he asked his old schoolmate Oliver Tambo to join him in the practice. Tambo was a brilliant law student and was committed to civil rights. The partners opened a practice in downtown Johannesburg. Black

Mandela at his Johannesburg law firm

clients flocked to the office. Every morning, the two lawyers had to wade through long lines of waiting clients just to open their doors. Mandela later explained why black South Africans needed so much assistance:

> Africans were desperate for legal help . . . it was a crime to walk through a Whites Only door, a crime to ride a Whites Only bus, a crime to use a

Whites Only drinking fountain, a crime to walk on a Whites Only beach, a crime to be on the streets after eleven, a crime not to have a pass book and a crime to have the wrong signature in that book, a crime to be unemployed and a crime to be employed in the wrong place, a crime to live in certain places and a crime to have no place to live.

Mandela and Tambo quickly discovered that the practice of the law on behalf of blacks in South Africa was an act of defiance in itself.

The partners turned out to be an excellent match. Tambo, a quiet and patient man, was the workhorse of the firm. Mandela, with a more flamboyant speaking

Oliver Tambo

style, was the perfect trial attorney. Together, they earned respect from the courts and other attorneys. Had they lived in a less oppressive country, they may have led simple lives of quiet comfort. But that was not to be.

Eventually, the partners were forced to move their offices, since they were set up in an area designated for whites only. It was harder for clients to reach the new offices on the outskirts of the city, and the move hurt the business considerably.

BURDENS OF THE STRUGGLE

By 1953, the Mandela marriage had gotten rocky. Nelson loved his family and was a dedicated father, but his schedule often took him away from home. Even when he was in town, he worked long hours and increasingly became a stranger to his family.

About the same time, Evelyn became a Jehovah's Witness. She embraced her new religion with a passion that matched Nelson's zeal for politics. But the change created a rift between the couple that grew day by day. Evelyn felt that her husband should put his faith in God and worry less about the fight for equality. He believed that a religious life had merit, but he wasn't willing to give up politics for it.

Nelson and Evelyn found themselves on entirely different paths and divorced in 1955. Nelson maintained a strong relationship with his children, and he missed the life of a married man. But he could grieve the loss of his marriage for only so long. The movement called, and he continued to answer it.

The government in Pretoria continued to reshape South African society according to the ideals of the Nationalist Party. In 1953, it passed the Bantu [black] Education Act, which ended funding for the religious schools that had educated blacks like Mandela. The law was obviously designed to keep the black population as ignorant as possible. The minister of Bantu Education, Dr. Hendrik Verwoerd, made that clear in a statement published shortly after the law was passed: "[Education] must train and teach people in accordance with their opportunities in life. . . . There is no place for the [black] in the European community above the level of certain forms of labor."

That year, a number of black communities responded to the law by boycotting government-run schools and setting up alternative schools called "culture clubs." These schools were independent and couldn't be controlled by the government. Soon Verwoerd declared that the alternative schools were illegal.

Black leaders were outraged and renewed their struggle. Under the new leadership of Albert Luthuli, the ANC organized a People's Congress. It drew delegates from all over the country and from all different ethnic groups. Even some sympathetic whites were a part of the first meeting, which took place in June 1955 in the small multiracial village of Kliptown, a few miles southwest of Johannesburg.

More than 3,000 people took part. They arrived by car, bus, truck, and even on foot. There was also a small army of police around, snapping pictures and recording the events in small notebooks.

The gathering was a fantastic sight. Songs were sung in Zulu, Xhosa, and English. There were dozens of impassioned speeches designed to create a sense of unity. But the real work of the two-day conference was the drafting of the Freedom Charter. It called for a radically different South Africa in which: "The People Shall Govern. All National Groups Shall Have Equal Rights. The People Shall Share In The Country's Wealth. The Land Shall Be Shared Among Those Who Work It. . . . "

The charter was a revolutionary document and was hotly debated by delegates who feared its Communist tone. Eventually, most delegates were pleased with the document, but they never got to vote on it. On the second day of the conference, police charged the speaker's platform, pushing delegates off the stage and accusing them of treason.

The authorities successfully broke up the conference, but they did not stop the world from taking notice and declaring the conference one of the most remarkable political gatherings of modern times.

Within three months, the government responded to the People's Congress. Invoking the Suppression of Communism Act, the police arrested anyone suspected of opposing government policies. In December 1956,

The Freedom Charter was written in English, Sotho, and Xhosa. Among the authors were ANC president Albert Luthuli, upper left, *and Mandela's mentor Walter Sisulu,* third from lower left.

Mandela was arrested again. He, along with 155 others, was to be placed on trial for high treason.

While the arrests were meant to silence dissent, they accomplished just the opposite. Because of banning orders, people who had been unable to talk with one another outside of prison now found themselves together in large cells. Old friends and comrades became reacquainted, while younger activists listened and learned. Instead of the sad desperation that often overtakes those in jail, there was an air of celebration. The people began to realize a power that the government could not contain with its guns and batons.

Not long after the arrests, the prisoners were released. But they were under strict banning orders until their trials. They could not travel or speak in
public. Mandela was a primary target of such orders,
as were others in high command of the ANC.

Even with the banning orders, the ANC leadership
called for a stay-at-home action in June of 1957. As a
form of protest, black people were instructed not to
go to work. The action was a remarkable success. In
some places, sixty to eighty percent of the black work-
force stayed off the job for several days.

REVOLUTIONARY LOVE

In the fall of 1957, Mandela put his time and energy
into the upcoming treason trials. If the men were
found guilty, they faced lengthy prison terms and a
substantial blow to the movement. Those thoughts
weighed heavily on Mandela's mind as he negotiated
the traffic of downtown Johannesburg one day.

As he passed the finest black hospital in the city,
there, standing at the bus stop, was a beautiful young
woman. He could not help craning his neck to get a
better look at her. Mandela was surprised by his interest in the woman. His marriage had fallen apart
largely because of his involvement in the ANC. Without actually admitting it, he had resigned himself to
the lonely life of a freedom fighter. If he did have a
marriage, it was to the struggle.

Still, the woman on the corner made him feel like a

A beaming Nelson and Winnie on their wedding day, 1958

boy of sixteen. Her eyes, her face, her bearing made him want to stop and talk. But there were other matters that required his attention. He scolded himself for thinking he had the luxury of romance at this point and drove on by.

Over the next few weeks, he found himself thinking about the woman at the bus stop. Somehow, her face had etched itself in his memory. That was why he was so amazed one day when he saw the woman seated in the office of his partner, Oliver Tambo. She and her brother were there to discuss a legal problem.

Mandela listened to what they had to say, but he had a hard time taking it in. He thought about the woman's eyes, her face, and her lips. About the only thing that stuck in his memory was her name, Nomzamo Winifred Madikizela. It meant "going through trials, one who strives." He knew in an instant the signs of love, and he didn't fight the feeling. Instead, he asked "Winnie" on a date. Had he been a high school student, he could not have been more infatuated.

On their first date, Nelson talked about the pending treason case and his life in the struggle. He also told her that he wanted to marry her. It is doubtful that Winnie took this mention of marriage seriously. However, the couple began to see one another regularly. She met his children, watched him work out at the gym, and accompanied him on many activities. To his delight, he quickly discovered that Winnie was as committed to the liberation of black South Africans as he was. Within a year, on June 15, 1958, the couple married.

Winnie's parents were proud to have such a famous and respected man in their family. Still, Winnie's father warned her that she was not just marrying a man. She was marrying the ANC as well. He also warned that she might be criticized for marrying a divorced man. Traditional African society frowned on divorce, particularly for those connected to royalty, as was Mandela.

From the beginning, Winnie and Nelson's lives were dominated by politics. To even get married, Nelson had to apply for a temporary relaxation of the banning orders that restricted his travel. He was allowed to leave Johannesburg for less than a week, to travel to the Transkei for the wedding.

ON TRIAL FOR TREASON

The Mandelas did not have much of a honeymoon. The treason trial formally opened the same month they were married. Charges had been dismissed against most of the original 156 protesters. But charges stood against thirty of the most prominent figures, including Mandela, who sat in jail while the trial proceeded.

In the midst of the high-profile trial, unrest continued in the black townships. In a peaceful protest at a train station in 1960, a group of blacks refused to present their passbooks, or identification papers, to police. Sixty-nine people were killed and another 180 wounded when police opened fire. The incident was called the Sharpeville massacre. The world condemned the incident, as by now it had a number of other outrages by the South African government.

The black community responded with more protests. In retaliation, the government declared a state of emergency, which allowed authorities to further suspend the rights of blacks and make even more arrests. Again, the crackdown had just the opposite effect of

The Sharpeville massacre caught the world's attention.

what was intended. With more of its leaders in jail, the ANC had a chance to plan new actions. The group selected Mandela to lead the ANC during the next phase of the struggle.

In the treason trial, the state tried to prove that the ANC was a Communist organization, bent on establishing a Communist government in South Africa. The state took several years to develop its case and racked up a small fortune in legal expenses. But in the end, on March 29, 1961, the defendants were found not guilty.

As the defendants left the courthouse they were greeted by enthusiastic crowds who cheered and sang *Nkosi Sikelel' iAfrika*. Mandela was pleased with the outcome of the trial, but he had no illusions about the future. He knew that the authorities were going to work harder next time to make sure that the activists stayed in jail.

Out of the country illegally, Mandela, left, and fellow activist
Robert Resha, third from left, met with leaders of the Algerian
army during their 1962 tour of Africa and Europe.

Chapter **SEVEN**

THE BLACK PIMPERNEL

IN **1961** THE BANNING ORDERS THAT HAD HAM-pered Mandela off and on for nearly a decade ran out. He had his public voice back, but he went underground to preserve it. With a frustrated police force frantic to keep an eye on him, Mandela began the bittersweet life of a fugitive.

For the first time in years, he traveled to the countryside. His banning orders had restricted him to Johannesburg for so long that he had nearly forgotten the natural beauty of rural South Africa. He met with rural activists and with journalists to explain his positions and argue his points. He wrote letters to students, who were by then becoming a powerful force in the struggle.

Mandela worked closely with his old friend and mentor Walter Sisulu. Mandela later noted that the older man gave him a sense of calm that enabled him to discuss his ideas with even the harshest critics without losing his temper—or the argument.

Mandela was invisible to the authorities, but his presence was felt in nearly every part of the country. The police conducted a massive manhunt, but Mandela continued to elude them. By now he and Winnie had two daughters, Zenani and Zindziswa. He visited them whenever possible, usually slipping in and out late at night. There were a few close calls, but he managed to stay one step ahead of the police.

His courage and daring were legendary in the black townships, and people renamed him "the Black Pimpernel"—a label inspired by a literary hero who saves others from danger. Mandela sparked hope in a generation of black youth while at the same time infuriating the South African government.

It was during this period that Mandela and a small number of ANC members formed a radical group called Umkhonto we Sizwe (Spear of the Nation). Since its establishment in 1912, the ANC had engaged in only nonviolent protests. But in situation after situation, peaceful protest had been met with police violence and further erosion of the rights of the black majority. Spear of the Nation resolved to try another tactic.

Setting up headquarters at a farm in a suburb of Johannesburg, the group decided to engage in acts of

WOMEN ARISE AND ACT!

The need for unity is the need for People's Power. It is the power against ignorance and general abuse. The search for active unity is the task for both men and women alike. Forward with the year of the women!

JOIN UMKHONTO WE SIZWE

Women were encouraged to join the radical group, Umkhonto we Sizwe.

sabotage against property and the economy. These actions were designed to put pressure on the government to make changes. But the leaders were careful to plan acts that would not harm people. They worked out the details of their plans during September, October, and November of 1961. Mandela lived at the farm during this period and was also able to spend some happy moments with his wife and children.

Ironically, just as the ANC was moving toward limited acts of violence, the world paid homage to its nearly fifty years of nonviolence. In early December 1961, former ANC president Albert Luthuli became the first African to be awarded the Nobel Prize for Peace. Within a week, on December 16, Spear of the Nation launched bomb attacks on sites in Johannesburg, Port Elizabeth, and Durban.

One Spear of the Nation member was killed in the explosions, which rocked white South Africa to its very foundations. Finally, liberals and moderates began to listen to the problems of the black majority, while the government prepared itself for an internal war.

That same month, the ANC received an invitation to attend the Pan African Freedom Movement conference in Addis Ababa, Ethiopia. The conference would unite leaders from all over Africa. The ANC decided to send Nelson Mandela as its representative. But he was not sure that he should go.

Mandela had earlier announced that he would not leave the country in such a time of danger. If African blood was to be spilled, he said, his would mingle with the rest. But Albert Luthuli and the others finally convinced Mandela to go. In January 1962, he sadly said good-bye to Winnie and his children and slipped out of the country.

In addition to attending the Pan African conference, Mandela toured East, West, and North Africa like a head of state. He visited the heads of African nations that had only recently thrown off the colonial yoke. He exchanged ideas with men who would lead their countries in the years to come. He received military training in Algeria, a country that had won independence from France barely two years earlier. Other African leaders were sympathetic to Mandela's cause. Some lent financial support, while others committed themselves to training ANC members.

Mandela then traveled to England and found a number of politicians within the Labor and Liberal Parties willing to discuss the situation in South Africa. He created quite a stir wherever he traveled, and the media took notice. All the while, his opponents in Pretoria watched from afar and waited.

After roughly seven months of travel, Mandela made good on his promise not to abandon South Africa. He returned to the country of his birth. He was happy to see his family and friends again, but he was also sad. South Africa had not changed in his absence. The white government continued to brutally oppress.

Back home, the Black Pimpernel again took up the life of a hunted fugitive. By now he had become a kind of Robin Hood to blacks, Indians, coloreds, and even whites who believed in democracy. To the government, he was an embarrassment, an unwelcome symbol of resistance, and the most dangerous man in the country. In early August 1962, the police got a tip on where they might find Mandela, and they closed in.

TRIAL AND IMPRISONMENT

Mandela had become a legend. He had traveled and made connections all over the world and could have easily remained in comfortable exile. Undoubtedly, the authorities would have welcomed that. They might even have allowed his family to join him out of the country.

Yet Mandela was a different sort of leader. He recalled the history of his people and his heritage within

Thembu royalty. He recalled the iron-fisted injustice for which Pretoria was famous and knew he could not save his people and himself at the same time. He would be there with them and make whatever sacrifice was necessary. After nearly seventeen months on the run, Mandela was arrested and put in a prison called the Johannesburg Fort. He was charged with inciting people to strike and with leaving the country illegally.

South Africa's minister of justice during that time was John Vorster, a man who had been jailed during World War II for his pro-Nazi views. During his term in office, he greatly limited freedom of speech and protest. He also helped pass the Sabotage Act, increasing penalties for trespassing, illegal possession of weapons, and other crimes. The minister also made banning more severe. Under the new laws, a banned person could not publish writings, receive visitors, or broadcast statements. Banned people had to report regularly to the police.

As restrictions tightened within South Africa, criticism of apartheid mounted on a global scale. The world had begun to condemn South Africa, and its government felt like it was under siege. It became defensive and prepared to do battle. Mandela was the symbol of a new national threat, and the government seemed determined to deal with him as such.

At the hearing following his arrest, Mandela noticed many familiar faces in the courtroom. He knew the judge and some of the lawyers from his years of practicing law. He also noticed that they seemed uneasy, even ashamed, when the hearing started. Here he was, labeled the most dangerous and wanted fugitive in South Africa—an outlaw of the highest order—but the lawyers treated him with professional courtesy and respect. He was Nelson Mandela, attorney-at-law, as far as they were concerned. It dawned on Mandela that these people saw him as an ordinary man being punished for his beliefs—beliefs that they knew to be honorable.

With that revelation, Mandela shook off the depression he had felt over his loss of freedom. He began to see that the world perceived him as a symbol of justice in the court of a tyrant. This feeling would grow in the coming weeks leading up to the actual trial.

Mandela planned to conduct his own defense. But he also enlisted the help of lawyer and Communist Party member Joe Slovo in preparing his case. Then, the trial was moved to Pretoria, and Slovo had to be replaced. A banning order restricted him to Johannesburg.

On October 15, 1962, Mandela's trial began in Pretoria. The guardians of the old order felt they finally had him where they wanted him. They thought they would silence him, humble him, and ultimately break him.

But the old freedom fighter had something else in mind. Had the authorities forgotten that he was a lawyer who thrived on trials? He was exactly where he needed to be. Throngs of supporters and journalists gathered from around the world. Everyone sensed that something monumental was about to take place, but few would have predicted what they were about to see.

As the trial opened, Mandela strode proudly into the packed Pretoria courtroom wearing a traditional Xhosa leopard-skin kaross, or cape, an outfit he would wear throughout the trial. He looked like a Xhosa king walking into a royal kraal for a coronation.

"Amandla" ("Power"), someone shouted and thrust a clenched fist into the air. *"Ngawethu"* ("The power is ours"), another voice intoned. Then, nearly everyone in the gallery rose and chanted until the pounding of the

Nelson Mandela found power in wearing traditional Xhosa attire during his trial.

Winnie Mandela also arrived at the trial in Xhosa dress.

magistrate's gavel silenced them. Winnie was among them. She was also dressed in Xhosa attire, which brought a smile to her husband's face.

Nelson Mandela wanted the world to know that this was not the trial of one man. He was not alone. Accompanying him into the courtroom were the ancestors of the freedom movement. Although invisible to the judge and guards, Mandela felt their presence. Xhosa King Ngangelizwe, who had fought the British in the nineteenth century, was there. Beside him walked Sekhukhne, king of the Bapedi; Moshoeshoe, the Basotho king; and Dingane, king of the Zulu. Their courage flowed through Mandela as he went to do battle in the way he knew best. He would use the trial to air grievances that were decades, if not centuries, old. Mandela intended to put the country itself on trial.

The battle did not actually begin that day. Mandela requested and was granted more time to prepare his case. He had thrown down the gauntlet, but it would be a week before an actual exchange would take place.

Mandela returned to court on October 22, 1962, and immediately took the offensive. He called for the judge to excuse himself from the case on the grounds that he was biased against the defendant. In fact, Mandela questioned whether the court had the right to hear the case at all. After all, as a black man, Mandela had no representative or voice in the South African government. He asked how that same government could expect him to abide by its laws. He went on to outline the rights that whites monopolized. He pointed out numerous ways in which blacks were kept on the bottom of society. In such an atmosphere, he questioned whether the court could give him a fair trial:

> Why is it that in this courtroom I am facing a white magistrate, confronted by a white prosecutor, escorted by white orderlies? Can anybody honestly and seriously suggest that in this type of atmosphere the scales of justice are evenly balanced? Why is it that no African in the history of this country has ever had the honor of being tried by his own kind, by his own flesh and blood? . . . I am a black man in a white man's court. This should not be.

The judge remained unpersuaded and ordered the case to move forward.

The prosecutor, Bob Bosch, was another lawyer who respected Mandela for his previous legal work. Nonetheless, he presented a vigorous case, calling more than one hundred witnesses. Mandela was no less aggressive as he questioned the witnesses on cross-examination. He pressed them hard, which often resulted in tense exchanges. But by the time the prosecution rested, there was strong evidence to show that Mandela had indeed left the country illegally and had incited workers to strike.

It was then the defense's turn to present its case. Surprisingly, Mandela announced that he would call no witnesses. He further announced he was resting his case. The judge, prosecutor, and spectators were shocked, and whispers rippled through the gallery. The prosecutor fumbled for words. He had not expected to present his closing argument so quickly. Finally, he simply asked the court to find the defendant guilty on both counts, and the court went into a short recess.

It was during the recess that prosecutor Bosch paid Mandela a surprise visit. Bosch apologized to him, explaining that he hated what he was doing, hated having to send Mandela to prison. Bosch then extended his hand. It is likely that most people in that situation would have given the prosecutor a piece of their mind. Mandela, however, accepted the handshake and thanked Bosch for his words.

When the court session began again, the judge summed up the charges and asked if Mandela had any

Crowds gathered outside the courthouse to show their support for the accused.

closing remarks. He certainly did—he spoke for nearly an hour. He never denied that he had traveled outside the country without the government's permission. He never denied encouraging blacks to boycott work during the 1961 campaigns. But he maintained that he wasn't a criminal. "I have done my duty to my people and to South Africa," he said. "I have no doubt that posterity will pronounce that I was innocent and that the criminals that should have been brought before this court are the members of the government."

Ten minutes later, following another recess to consider the sentence, the judge returned and pronounced a sentence of five years in prison: three years for inciting people to strike and two years for leaving the country. In Port Elizabeth, acts of sabotage greeted the news of the conviction.

A day earlier, on November 6, 1962, the General Assembly of the United Nations had voted in favor of sanctions, or penalties, against South Africa for its human rights abuses. Some countries refused to do business with South Africa. They hoped to hurt South Africa economically as a way to pressure the government to make changes.

Mandela was to serve five years without the possibility of parole. This was a harsh sentence, and some people in the courtroom responded with wails and weeping. Without knowing for sure, Mandela felt Winnie must have been among them. The punishment would hurt her almost as much as him. Still, Mandela stood tall and proud. He raised a clenched fist to the gallery, and the crowd roared: *"Amandla! Amandla! Amandla!"*

The fervor of the crowd's response confirmed Mandela's feeling that his personal sacrifices were worth it. He was filled with a sense of love for the African people and all those who struggled to end the nightmare of apartheid. But what moved him to tears was the singing of the South African national anthem, *Nkosi Sikelel' iAfrika.*

Following the reading of the sentence, Winnie and her husband had only a few minutes to say good-bye. Despite the anguish she was feeling, she wore a brave face. There were no tears. She never lost sight of the fact that she was also a comrade in the struggle.

As Mandela was taken away in a police van, he heard the crowd of supporters singing *Nkosi Sikelel' iAfrika* in his honor. He held the face of Winnie in his mind and his spirits soared. However, soon other faces came to mind: his young children, Zenani and Zindziswa, as well as Thembelike and Makgatho from his first marriage. His longing for them was enough to make him weep.

Mandela went first to Pretoria Central Prison, but within a short time he was transferred to the notorious Robbens Island. The Island, as it was often called, was all too familiar to the Xhosa. The windswept rock, four miles off the coast of Cape Town, had been used as a prison since the Boers settled in Africa in the seventeenth century. The prison was set up to break the spirits of those who resisted the rule of the state.

Although there were white prisoners on the island, the worst treatment was reserved for black prisoners, especially those convicted of political crimes. Mandela's clothes were confiscated, and he was issued the standard attire for African prisoners: a pair of baggy shorts, a prison shirt, and sandals. He and the other African prisoners were not allowed to wear long pants like white prisoners, even in winter when the temperature often dipped below freezing. By dressing the black prisoners like children, the state meant to remind them that it indeed thought of blacks as such.

Some months after his arrival on the Island, Mandela was transferred back to Pretoria. He soon learned through the prison grapevine that other members of the ANC had been arrested and awaited trial on charges of sabotage for the Spear of the Nation bombings. The government wasted no time in blaming Mandela and charging him with sabotage, too.

The State versus Nelson Mandela and others was to be argued before the Supreme Court in the South African Palace of Justice. Not far from the entrance to the palace stood a statue of Paul Kruger, an Afrikaner founding father who fought against British rule in the nineteenth century. There was an inscription on the pedestal that read:

> In confidence we lay our cause before the world. Whether we win or die, freedom will rise in Africa like the sun from the morning clouds.

How things had changed. The once oppressed Afrikaners had become the oppressors. Still, as the police transport passed the statue, Mandela considered just how appropriate the words were for the struggle of blacks in his country.

I AM THE FIRST ACCUSED

"I am the first accused," Nelson Mandela said in his first public statement in over a year. It was the beginning of a lengthy statement that introduced the defense's case in the sabotage trial of April 1964.

Mandela explained that Spear of the Nation felt it had no course other than violent action. "All lawful modes of expressing opposition to this principle [apartheid] had been closed by legislation, and we were placed in a position in which we had either to accept a permanent state of inferiority, or defy the government," he said.

He went on to outline the history of the African National Congress. He explained how the ANC had first tried to work within the established political system, noting that even after basic rights had been stripped from black people, the ANC retained its nonviolent stance. He quoted Chief Albert Luthuli who had said:

> Who will deny that thirty years of my life have been spent knocking in vain, patiently, moderately, and modestly at a closed and barred door? What have been the fruits of moderation? The past thirty years have seen the greatest number of laws restricting our rights and progress, until today we have reached a stage where we have almost no rights.

Mandela explained that in 1949, the ANC had shifted its tactics somewhat, launching a Defiance Campaign of demonstrations and labor strikes. Although nearly 9,000 people had gone to jail during the campaign, it had remained nonviolent. And while the ANC had maintained its commitment to peaceful demonstrations over the years, the government had launched countless acts of violence against the people. Mandela continued before the judge:

Already, scores of Africans had died as a result of racial friction. In 1920 when the famous leader Masabala was held in Port Elizabeth jail, twenty-four of a group of Africans who had gathered to demand his release were killed by police and white civilians. In 1921, more than one hundred Africans died in the Bulhoek affair. In 1924 over two hundred Africans were killed when the Administrator of South-West Africa led a force against a group which had rebelled against the imposition of a dog tax. On May 1, 1950, eighteen Africans died as a result of police shootings during the strike. On March 21, 1960, sixty-nine unarmed Africans died at Sharpeville. How many more Sharpevilles would there be?. . . The hard facts were that fifty years of nonviolence had brought the African people nothing but more and more repressive legislation, and fewer and fewer rights. . . . It showed that a Government which uses force to maintain its rule teaches the oppressed to use force to oppose it.

Mandela's voice filled the courtroom as he laid out what most of white South Africa had never contemplated. He explained that the ANC leadership had agonized over how to proceed after nonviolent tactics had failed. They had begun to discuss their options, and out of that discussion they had formed Spear of the Nation. He quoted the group's manifesto:

The time comes in the life of any nation when there remain only two choices—submit or fight. That time has now come to South Africa. We shall not submit and we have no choice but to hit back by all the means in our power in defense of our people, our future, and our freedom.

Mandela explained that Spear of the Nation had chosen to commit sabotage—but sabotage that would cause no loss of life. He concluded:

During my lifetime I have dedicated myself to this struggle of the African people. I have fought against white domination, and I have fought against black domination. I cherished the ideal of a democratic and free society in which all persons live together in harmony and with equal opportunities. It is an ideal which I hope to live for and to achieve. But if needs be, it is an ideal for which I am prepared to die.

Mandela was eventually found guilty of four counts of sabotage and was sentenced to life in prison along with ANC members Walter Sisulu, Govan Mbeki, Raymond Mhlaba, Elias Motsoaledi, Andrew Mlangeni, Ahmed Kathrada, and Denis Goldberg.

BEHIND BARS

Now that Mandela was in the belly of the beast, the

government set out to accomplish two things. It would break his spirit and stamp out his memory. Once Mandela was out of circulation, the government figured people would become disheartened and forget about him.

But he was not so easily forgotten. Many grieved his imprisonment but none more than his wife, who was left to explain things to the children and to hold the family together. But Winnie knew that most black South African women faced similar burdens.

"Insofar as the black woman in South Africa is concerned, each black home is a political institution," Winnie later said. "There isn't a fiber of a black's life that is not intruded upon by the apartheid laws which are so brutal that they affect little children. . . . In our sick society, when a man hasn't been to prison, you look twice at that black man. It means that there is something wrong with that man."

Year after year, Mandela survived the rigors of prison life. Through most of it, Walter Sisulu was there enduring with him. Despite the hardships, Mandela kept up a routine of physical exercise—running

People all over the world, like these Londoners, protested on behalf of Mandela and his codefendants.

in place, sit-ups, and push-ups. He kept his mind sharp through study and, when possible, discussion. Even within the prison walls, news from the outside seeped in, and Mandela kept abreast of it.

The treatment of blacks in prison continued to resemble the treatment of blacks in the rest of society. White prisoners wore long pants while blacks wore shorts. Medical care and the quality of food differed substantially for blacks and whites, as well. Over time, conditions improved, but only as a result of prisoner hunger strikes, work slowdowns, and international pressure. Eventually, black prisoners won the right to

Prisoners, including Mandela in the front row, worked splitting rocks inside the Robbens Island courtyard.

Mandela's daughters, Zenani, left, *and Zindziswa,* right, *visit their father in prison.*

talk to one another and to have improved food, long pants, and more blankets.

The world had not forgotten about the freedom fighters held in captivity. Mandela's name became a rallying cry, and the social storm intensified. Brutal police attacks were commonplace, and the black townships became ungovernable. But the government refused to change course. With every new sign of unrest, the police cracked down with no concern for the truth.

By the mid-1970s, black students had stepped into the forefront of the struggle. Their work was similar to the student protests in the United States during the late 1960s and early 1970s. But unlike the U.S. government, the South African government treated protesters like enemies of the state.

Things came to a tragic head in 1976 when Afrikaans, the hated language of the Boers, became a required course in South African schools. Students at all levels reacted by boycotting school. The largest boycott took place in the Soweto township outside Johannesburg.

Protests began peacefully, but the government took its usual stance of tolerating no defiance. The police moved in on the township during what came to be called the Soweto uprising. During sixteen months of unrest, roughly one thousand people died and four thousand were injured. Most of those killed and injured were children. Thousands of students were jailed. Some spent up to five years in confinement, while others were never heard from again.

The reign of terror continued the next year. So did the resistance—especially as the notion of "Black Power" filtered in from civil rights activists in the United States. As quickly as the authorities could destroy one student leader, another would move to the forefront. The best-known student activist was Steven Biko. He was beaten to death in police custody. A young Indian named Ahmed Timol was killed in a fall from the tenth floor of police headquarters in Johannesburg. Other student leaders died mysteriously, while those who survived were hampered by banning orders.

All the while, the international community increased pressure on Pretoria. Many countries stepped up economic boycotts of South Africa, refusing to invest in

Thirteen-year-old Hector Peterson was the first person to die in the 1976 Soweto uprising.

South African companies or buy South African products. Since 1964, South Africa had been banned from the Olympics and other international competitions. The United Nations continued to condemn apartheid.

Bit by bit, it became apparent to the South African government that something had to be done. It was obvious that the one man capable of resolving the situation sat in prison for life. The only sane course seemed to be the release of Nelson Mandela from prison and the opening of the political process to all South Africans. However, it would take the right leader to bring about the change.

Nelson and Winnie Mandela raise their fists, signifying African solidarity, as Nelson leaves prison after twenty-seven years.

Chapter **EIGHT**

FREE AT LAST

ON JULY 4, 1989, WHILE AMERICANS CELE-
brated Independence Day, Nelson Mandela was informed by prison officials that he was to meet with
the South African president, P. W. Botha, the next day.
Realizing that Mandela in prison was as much a political force as he was outside, earlier administrations
had tried several times to get him out—if they could
only get him to do their bidding. They had pressured
Mandela to renounce the use of violence and illegal
protests. Time and again, however, Mandela had
found the government's terms unacceptable and had
elected to remain in prison. He wondered if things
would be different this time.

Known to have a fierce temper, President Botha was

nicknamed "the Great Crocodile." He was more inclined to dictate to black leaders than to talk with them. So Mandela was surprised that the meeting turned out to be a friendly one. The two men spent much of the time discussing South African history, though from very different points of view. Finally, Mandela directed the conversation to more important matters. He explained that there could be no real negotiations until political prisoners were released unconditionally.

Not surprisingly, Botha informed Mandela that the government could not meet his terms. In fact, the meeting ended with no real resolution. Nonetheless, Mandela felt good about it. He realized that all the pressure and social unrest were finally taking their toll. It would be only a short time before his dream of a new South Africa would become a reality.

Things became less certain, however, when Botha resigned from office a month later. The resignation threw the ongoing negotiations between Mandela and the government into a quandary. A cabinet member, F. W. de Klerk, was sworn in as acting president. He was an unknown and nothing in his past suggested that he'd be any more sympathetic to the black cause than others in the government had been. Still, negotiations continued.

Mandela held firm to his demands. As de Klerk was sworn in as president, Mandela again requested that all political prisoners be released. In exchange for a democratic and racially free South Africa, Mandela promised disciplined behavior from the black leadership.

Mandela watched the new president and sized him up. He was made hopeful by what he saw. When faced with a demonstration, de Klerk did not ban the leaders as his predecessors had. He simply instructed the leaders to make the demonstration peaceful. That, in itself, was a change.

Finally, in October of 1989, de Klerk did something Mandela had waited nearly three decades to see. He released a number of political prisoners. Among them was Mandela's longtime friend and mentor, Walter Sisulu. That action laid the foundation for a meeting between the president and Mandela on December 12.

Unlike the meeting with Botha, this one actually bore fruit. The two men did not always see eye-to-eye, but de Klerk was someone with whom Mandela could do business. Mandela later described de Klerk as a thoughtful man who was willing to listen and think matters through. He made none of the knee-jerk reactions Mandela had come to expect from authorities.

One point that stood as an obstacle, however, was the president's idea of "group rights." This concept would essentially preserve power for white South Africans, regardless of election outcomes. Mandela would not accept this idea. It looked to him like the government was not really willing to end apartheid—only to modify it.

After some thought, de Klerk acknowledged that the government's position could be adjusted. On February 2, 1990, he made it clear that he was sincere. Before

Parliament, he announced sweeping changes that would dismantle apartheid. He announced that the government would lift the bans on the ANC, the Communist Party, and the Pan African Congress, as well as thirty-one other organizations. The government would also free political prisoners, suspend capital punishment, and lift other restrictions.

A week later, de Klerk was back with Mandela, explaining that he would be released from prison the next day. There would be no restrictions placed on Mandela; he would be free to continue his political activity.

On February 11, 1990, after twenty-seven years in prison, Nelson Mandela was free. In the great square in front of City Hall in Cape Town, a throng of people greeted him. There was thunderous applause as Mandela stepped to the microphone, his wife Winnie at his side, and raised his fist in victory. *"Amandla,"* he shouted. *"Ngawethu,"* the crowd called back.

The air was charged with excitement and power. The hero of the African liberation struggle stood before the crowd. Generations had grown up without seeing his face, only hearing his name in whispers. Now here he was, older yes, but fit, trim, and full of life.

"Friends, comrades, and fellow South Africans," he started in a clear voice. These were the first public words he had uttered since his trial decades earlier. "I greet you all in the name of peace, democracy and freedom for all. I stand before you not as a prophet but as a humble servant of you, the people."

He saluted the people and the various groups that had worked to end the injustice of apartheid. He praised all who had fought and died in the struggle. He praised the heroism of students who had resisted when their parents no longer had the will to fight. He praised his comrades in the ANC and other organizations that had worked for justice. He also praised the international community for its sanctions against South Africa:

Today the majority of South Africans, black and white, recognize that apartheid has no future. It has to be ended by our own decisive mass action in order to build peace and security. . . . The destruction caused by apartheid on our subcontinent is incalculable. The fabric of family life of millions of my people has been shattered. Millions are homeless and unemployed. Our economy lies in ruins and our people are embroiled in political strife. . . . The factors which necessitated the armed struggle still exist today. We have no option but to continue. We express the hope that a climate conducive to a negotiated settlement will be created soon so that there may no longer be the need for the armed struggle.

Mandela went on to Soweto and greeted another massive gathering in the soccer stadium there. Many in the audience were youths who had witnessed the protests in and around their township. They, too, lifted the spirits of their hero with the sound of their cheers.

Shortly after the fanfare surrounding his release had died down, Mandela reported to the ANC leadership about the state of negotiations with the government. Members of the Executive Committee were pleased to see him free, but there were questions in their eyes. They wondered if Mandela was the same man who had gone to prison. Had he been broken? Had he sold out? Mandela understood the questions. He had been isolated for a long time. But he put the leaders' fears to rest, and by the end of the meeting he was elected deputy president of the ANC.

Having regained the confidence of his colleagues, Mandela went abroad and met with leaders through-out Africa, Europe, and America. He was amazed at the enthusiastic responses wherever he went. Even the most conservative leaders, those who had criticized the ANC in the past, welcomed him. They were im-pressed with him not only for his conviction and great intellect but also for his lack of bitterness toward those who had imprisoned him. Mandela did not fo-cus on revenge but only upon what was best for the future of his country.

Unfortunately, while his public life was a series of successes, his family life was difficult. Winnie was on a different political track. As Nelson worked to bring all South Africans together, Winnie was more con-frontational toward the government. Her brand of radicalism seemed counterproductive to many within the ANC. The couple had also drifted apart in personal ways. In April 1992, Mandela announced that he and Winnie had separated. He was careful to explain that he still loved and respected her.

In a painful revelation, Mandela realized that he was married to the struggle and was father to a nation. He regretted the pain his family had experienced. But apartheid had destroyed the lives and families of millions of others, as well. Though his sacrifices were great, they had to be made if a new nation were to come into being.

Throughout his personal difficulties, Mandela stayed on course politically. He negotiated with the government to create a new political structure. Negotiations were not always easy. Radical forces on both sides tried to disrupt the process. However, on June 3, 1993, Mandela presented a formula for a new political system that gave rights to all South Africans. The first national, racially unrestricted, one-person-one-vote election would be held the following year.

It was a historic turning point. Mandela and President de Klerk were both rewarded for their efforts later in 1993, when they jointly accepted the Nobel Prize for Peace. As they stood together in Oslo, Norway, Mandela applauded de Klerk's efforts as a partner in moving the nation beyond the dark past of racial hatred.

Ironically, the two men who raised hands together in

An extraordinary moment in world history—Mandela and de Klerk receive the 1993 Nobel Peace Prize.

Oslo then became political rivals back home. The dismantling of apartheid prompted the first election in which all South Africans could participate. The black majority finally had a say in the running of their country, and the man they wanted for president was Nelson Mandela. On May 2, 1994, Mandela won the election and became the first black president of South Africa. He made it his duty to heal the wounds of the past.

"This is one of the most important moments in the life of our country," he said during his victory speech. "I stand here before you filled with deep pride and joy—pride in the ordinary, humble people of this country. You have shown such a calm, patient determination to reclaim this country as your own, and now the joy that we can loudly proclaim from the rooftops—Free at last! Free at last! I stand before you, humbled by your courage, with a heart full of love for all of you. . . . This is a time to heal the old wounds and build a new South Africa."

A week later, as Nelson Mandela was being sworn into office, he looked out upon a sea of faces. There

Mandela casts his presidential ballot.

In April 1994, thousands lined up to vote in South Africa's first racially unrestricted election.

were leaders from around the world, journalists, and comrades in the struggle. All looked on as this man of dignity and strength took the oath of office and addressed the crowd:

> Out of the experience of an extraordinary human disaster that lasted too long, must be born a society of which all humanity will be proud. . . . We have, at last, achieved our political emancipation. We pledge ourselves to liberate all our people from the continuing bondage of poverty, deprivation, suffering, gender, and other discrimination. Never, never, and never again shall it be that this beautiful land will again experience the oppression of one by another. . . . The sun shall never set on so glorious a human achievement.
> Let freedom reign. God bless Africa!

SOURCES

8–9   "Nelson Mandela's Inauguration Speech" Online. Available Gopher:
      //gopher.anc.org.za. March 10, 1998.
12   Nelson Mandela, *Long Walk to Freedom: The Autobiography of Nelson
      Mandela*, paperback ed. (Boston: Little, Brown, 1986), 5.
16–17 Vusamazulu C. Mutwa, *Africa is My Witness* (Cambridge, Mass.: Blue
      Crane, 1966), 297.
27   Mandela, *Long Walk to Freedom*, 19.
30–31 Ibid., 26.
34–35 Ibid., 32.
36   Ibid., 36.
47   Ibid., 64.
47   Ibid.
57   Mandela, *Long Walk to Freedom*, 95.
58   Ibid., 110.
59   Mary Benson, *Nelson Mandela: The Man and the Movement* (New York:
      W.W. Norton, 1986), 48.
63–64 Mandela, *Long Walk to Freedom, 130.*
66   Ibid., 145.
84   Ibid., 326.
86   Ibid., 332.
89–92 "I am Prepared to Die" Online. ANC Gopher site.
93   Benson, *Nelson Mandela: The Man and the Movement, 297.*
102–103 "Nelson Mandela's Address On His Release From Prison" Online. ANC
      Gopher site.
106–107 "Nelson Mandela's Election Victory Speech" Online. ANC Gopher site.
108   "Nelson Mandela's Inauguration Speech" Online. ANC Gopher site.

BIBLIOGRAPHY

Benson, Mary. *Nelson Mandela: The Man and the Movement.* New York: W.W.
   Norton, 1986.
Denenberg, Barry. *Nelson Mandela: "No Easy Walk to Freedom."* New York:
   Scholastic, 1991.
Hughs, Libby. *Nelson Mandela Speaks: Forging a Democratic, Nonracial South Africa.*
   New York: Pathfinder, 1993.
Mandela, Nelson. *Long Walk to Freedom: The Autobiography of Nelson Mandela,*
   paperback ed. Boston: Little, Brown, 1986.
Mandela, Nelson. *Struggle is My Life.* New York: Pathfinder, 1986.
Mutwa, C. Vusamazulu. *Africa is My Witness.* Cambridge, Mass.: Blue Crane, 1966.
Nelson Mandela's Speeches. Online. Available Gopher: //gopher.anc.org.za. March 10,
   1998.

INDEX

PRONUNCIATION GUIDE

Afrikaans	ah-free-KAHNS
Albert Luthuli	loo-TOO-lee
Amandla	ah-MAHNJ-lah
apartheid	ah-PAHR-tayd
Jongintaba	jun-geen-TAH-bah
kaross	KEH-rohs
Mfecane	m-feh-GAH-nee
Mfengu	m-FENG-goo
Mphakanyiswa	m-pah-gah-NEEZ-wah
Ngawethu	n-gah-WAY-too
Nkosi Sikelel' iAfrika	n-KOH-see sik-eh-LEH-lee ee-AH-free-kah
Nongqawuse	NUN-gow-OO-zay
P.W. Botha	BWEH-thah
Qunu	KOO-noo
Rolihlahla	ho-lee-SHAH-shah
Soweto	soh-WAY-toh
Thembu	TEM-boo
Transkei	trahn-SKY
Xhosa	KOH-sah

ABOUT THE AUTHOR

Reggie Finlayson is a modern-day griot—an oral historian of the West African tradition. In this role, he combines poetry, music, and storytelling to preserve the history of African and African-American people. Finlayson studied at Swarthmore College and at Marquette University, where he earned a master's degree in journalism. He is a member of the Ko-Thi African Dance Company and a teacher at the Milwaukee Area Technical College. He has written six plays, one of which is for children. This is his second biography for children.

PHOTO ACKNOWLEDGMENTS

The photographs and illustrations are reproduced with the permission of: American Lutheran Church, p. 97; AP/Wide World Photos, p. 83; Archive Photos/Express Newspapers, p. 94; Archive Photos/Juda Ngwenya/Reuters, p. 52; Archive Photos/Nordisk Pressefoto, p. 64; © David Brauchli/Sygma, p. 2; The McGregor Museum/The Duggan-Cronin Collection, p. 24; The McGregor Museum/The Aubrey Elliott Collection, p. 19; Mayibuye Centre/U.W.C., pp. 10, 27, 28, 32, 37, 39, 49, 51, 60, 63, 68, 70, 73, 74, 77, 82, 86, 93, 95; © National Archives of South Africa, #TAB 36025, p. 14; Reuters/Corbis-Bettmann, pp. 6, 98, 108; Reuters/Ulli Michel/Archive Photos, p. 106; Reuters/Phillipe Wojazer/Archive Photos, p. 107; UPI/Corbis-Bettmann, pp. 42, 45, 55, 61. Front cover photograph: Archive Photos/AMW Pressedienst. Back cover photograph: Mayibuye Centre/U.W.C.